Balloon Sculpting Tutorials

How to Make Balloon Animals for Beginners

© 2021 All rights reserved

Table of Content

INTRODUCTION _____ 3

HOW TO MAKE A DOG BALLOON ANIMAL _____ 4

HOW TO TWIST A BASIC BALLOON SWORD WITH EASE _____ 13

HOW TO MAKE A FLOWER BALLOON _____ 19

HOW TO MAKE A MONKEY BALLOON ANIMAL _____ 24

HOW TO MAKE A BALLOON BUTTERFLY _____ 32

HOW TO MAKE A BALLOON HAT _____ 37

HOW TO MAKE A BALLOON PENGUIN _____ 46

Introduction

If you want to entertain with balloon sculpting at a party, here are some tried and true creations that you should know how to make quickly and effortlessly.

These are suitable for parties of all ages, from the youngest school-age children. In general, you should practice for a while with some good quality balloons (not the kind you get at the party store) before you get in front of an audience.

Once you're feeling confident, you may want to add a little banter to your routine, chit-chat with people while you put their requested creation together. Of course, this is optional, but it can add an extra aspect of entertainment to the whole performance.

If you're performing for a group of kids, it's not a bad idea to make a few samples ahead of time, and display them at a table where you'll be doing your magic. That way, you don't get stuck with a kid asking you to make one that's not in your repertoire.

How to Make a Dog Balloon Animal

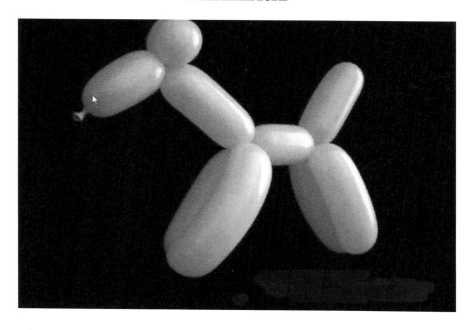

The dog balloon is a fundamental sculpture in the art of balloon twisting and balloon animals. And once you know how to make a dog, you can make a giraffe, wiener dog, and a mouse.

You'll start with three basic balloon twists. The first will be about two inches long, which will form the snout of the dog. The second and third twists will be smaller, about an inch each, to form the dog's ears.

What You'll Need

Materials: 1 260Q-size balloon

Instructions

1. Inflate the Balloon

First, inflate the balloon, leaving about 2 inches not inflated at the end. Tie off the open end.

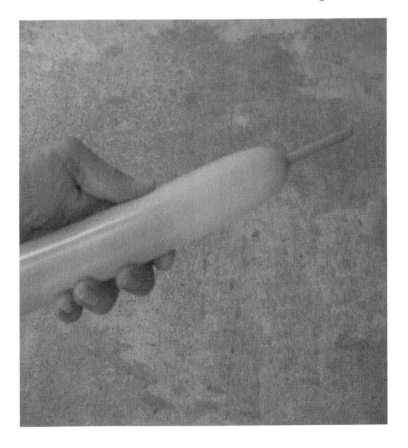

2. Make 3 Starting Twists

Twist three basic balloon twists at the end you tied off. The first should be about 2 inches long.

And the second and third twists should be slightly smaller at about 1 inch apiece.

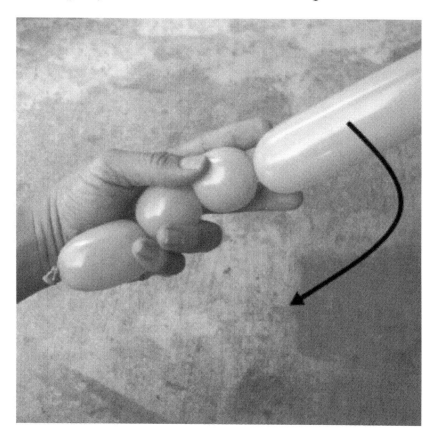

3. Form the Dog Snout and Ears

The first balloon twist (marked A in the photo below) will form the snout of the dog. The second and third twists (marked B and C) will form the dog's ears.

Bring twist A against the main body of the balloon in preparation for a lock twist. Then, twist B and C together while holding A and the main body of the balloon to create a lock twist.

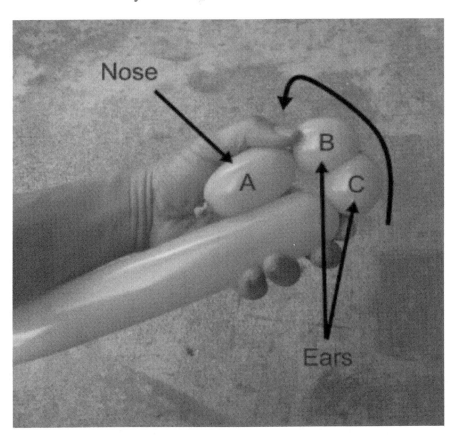

4. **Note the Dog's Head**

Your balloon sculpture should now resemble the head of a dog.

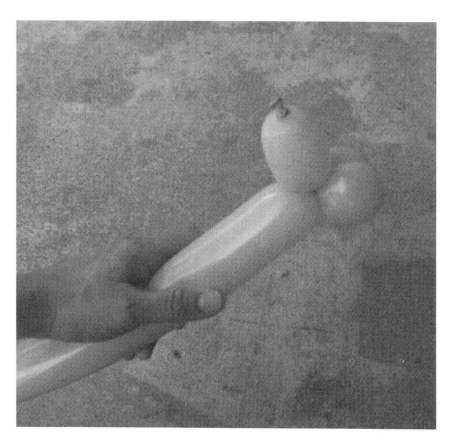

5. Form the Neck and Front Legs

Twist three basic balloon twists below the head, each about 3 inches long. The first segment (marked A in the photo below) will form the dog's neck. The second and third segments (marked B and C) will form the dog's front legs.

Next, as you did with the dog's head, create a lock twist by twisting B and C together while holding A against the body of the balloon.

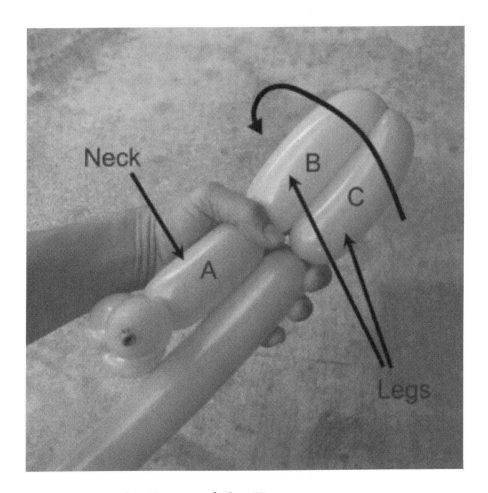

6. Note the Front of the Dog

Your twisted balloon sculpture should now resemble the front of a dog with its head and front legs.

7. Form the Body and Back Legs

Twist three basic balloon twists below the front legs, each about 3 inches long. The first segment (marked A in the photo below) will form the dog's body. The second and third twists (marked B and C) will form the dog's back legs. The final balloon segment (D) will form the dog's tail.

As you did with the dog's front legs, create a lock twist by twisting segments B and C together while holding segment A against segment D. Now, your dog should have back legs and a tail, completing your dog balloon animal.

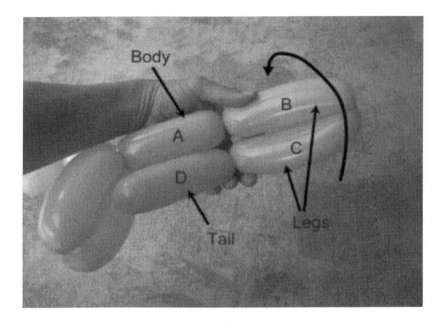

Tips for Making Dog Balloon Animals

Once you have the basic dog balloon animal down, you can try out some simple variations on the shape.

- Make the body segment extra long and the leg segments short to create a dachshund.
- Use a yellow balloon and create an extra-long neck segment to form a giraffe.

- Twist a relatively short neck and long legs, and you can call the balloon animal a horse.

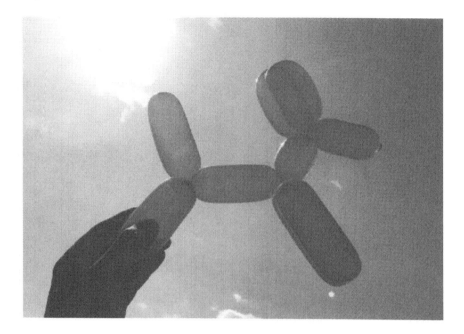

How to Twist a Basic Balloon Sword With Ease

Sword balloons are your basic, most straightforward balloon design. While technically not a balloon "animal," most kids will dig having a sword to play with. A good basic design starts with two balloons which you braid like challah bread, but there are a couple of variations you should try to learn.

What You'll Need

- ❖ **Equipment/Tools**
  1 Balloon pumper (optional, but helpful if blowing up many balloons)
- ❖ **Materials**

1 260-sized balloon

Instructions

These instructions are for a basic sword balloon with a hilt and straight shaft. It is easy to learn and twist. The main skill you need is the ability to create a fold twist. Once you master it, you may want to go on to make an ultimate sword balloon with a twisted shaft. Plus, you can learn to make a balloon scabbard that will hold the sword.

1. Inflate the Balloon

Inflate the balloon and tie it off, leaving a 1-inch uninflated tip at the end. You can use a balloon pumper or simply blow it up with your mouth. It is important to leave the tip because you are going to be twisting the balloon. If you inflate it fully, it will be overinflated when twisted and may burst.

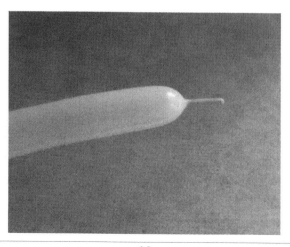

Tip

A 260-sized balloon is the most popular size for balloon animals. Be sure to get a high-quality balloon for the best results and endurance. If you have smaller hands or are making a sword for a smaller child, you might use the thinner 160 balloons. Likewise, you could choose the thicker 360 balloons for a beefier sword.

2. Start the Sword Handle

Make a basic twist about 5 inches from the balloon's knotted end. After twisting it, you will need to keep hold of it so it does not untwist.

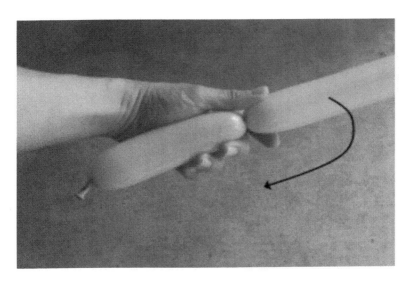

3. Continue the Handle With a Fold Twist

Bend the second segment of the balloon at about the 3-inch mark to make a fold twist. Create a fold twist. After folding the balloon 3 inches from the first twist, twist the folded segment with the first twist.

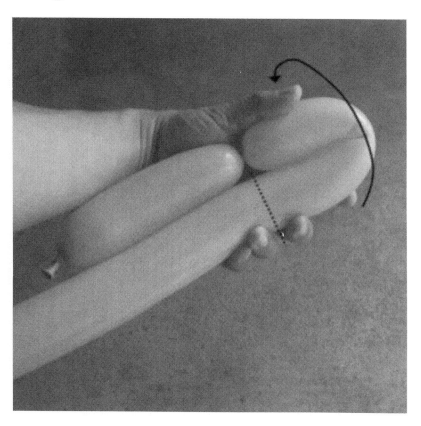

4. Look at the First Half of the Handguard

You have just twisted one-half of the handguard for the sword. You should have a short section of the handle, one-half of the handguard, and the long shaft.

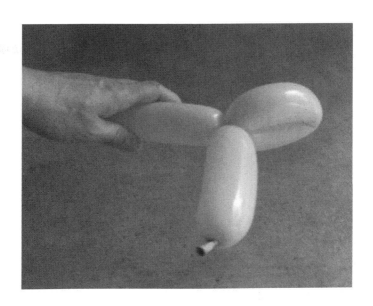

5. Fold the Second Part of the Handguard

Fold the balloon again 3 inches from the first fold. Twist a second fold twist the same size as the first one to create the second part of the handguard.

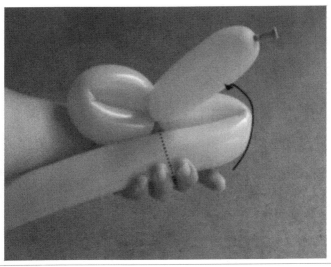

6. Finish the Sword Balloon

Once you straighten out the handguards so they are at right angles to the shaft of the balloon sword, you have completed twisting a balloon sword.

You will find that kids love these balloon swords. Kids will line up all day to get their hands on one.

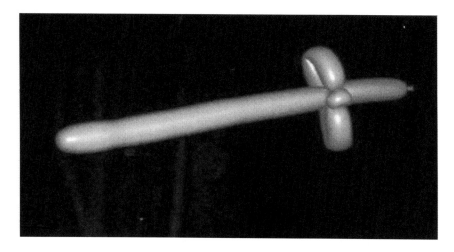

How to Make a Flower Balloon

Like the sword, the flower balloon is not really a balloon "animal" per se. But it is cute, and it is a crowd-pleaser. You'll want at least two 260 balloons (made specifically for twisting and designs) in different colors. You'll start with two loops on a twisted axis to make the petals (it sounds more intimidating than it is), and work in the "leaves" from there.

What You'll Need

- ❖ **Materials**
  2 260 balloons

Instructions

1. Inflate the Balloon

Inflate the balloon to about 2 inches from the end.

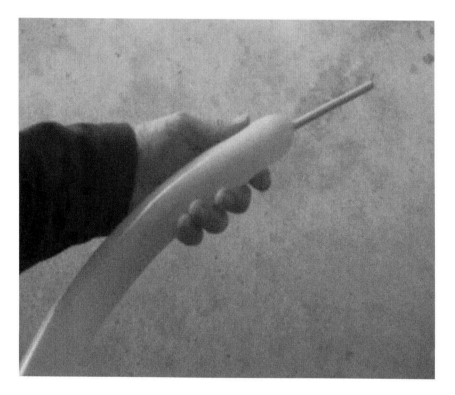

2. Make the Petals

Make a small fold twist using a balloon segment that is about 4 inches long. Repeat the process for another four petals, for a total of five, trying to make each one the same size as the first fold twist. Straighten out the five-fold twists so they form the petals of a flower. You're done with the petals.

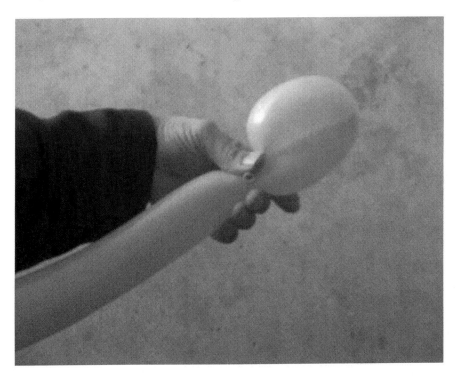

3. Make and Attach the Stem

Inflate the second (probably green) balloon and leave a 1/2 inch of the inflated balloon at the end.

Taking the nozzle end of the green balloon, make a small basic twist, about 1 inch in length. Join this basic twist to the center of the flower petals. To do this, stretch the basic twist away from the rest of the balloon (stem), and insert the flower, so the petals reside between the nozzle twist and the rest of the balloon.

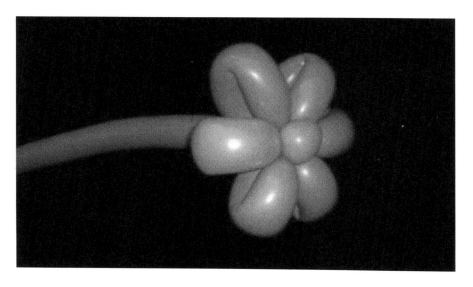

4. Finish the Center

At this point, you have three options for the center of the balloon flower:

1. **Leave the basic twist as-is.** When you join the "stem" to the petals of the flower, you'll have a nozzle showing in the middle of the flower. This is fine, but it's probably the least finished of the options. A plus, this is the fastest method to make a flower balloon if you're pressed for time or have lots of people waiting in line.
2. **Finish the basic twist after joining the stem to the flower.** Join the stem to the flower and then take the nozzle and wrap

it around the flower, in between the petals. You'll have a flower center that doesn't show the nozzle.

3. **Make a tulip twist in the flower's center.** Before joining the basic twist of the stem to the flower, make a tulip twist in the nozzle end. Attach the tulip twist to the flower petals as you did in option one.

5. **Add Leaves (Optional)**

If you like, you can add "leaves" by twisting the "stem" with a couple of fold twists as you would for a basic sword balloon. In this case, you're essentially making the handguard for the sword, but are forming "leaves." The technique to quickly make a handguard for a sword applies here to make the leaves.

How to Make a Monkey Balloon Animal

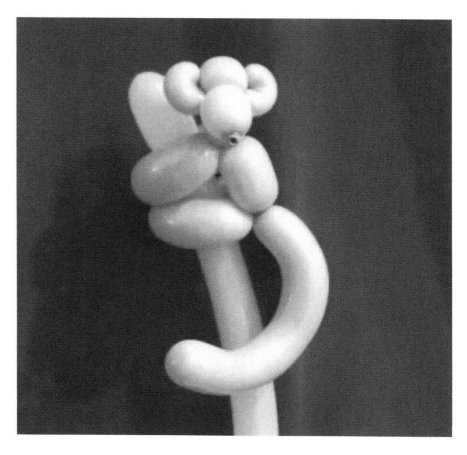

Here's a crowd-pleaser that deserves a spot in your repertoire. It's a monkey balloon animal. This one is not only fun and whimsical, it's cute and offers lots of opportunities for customization. This one is well worth learning and it's actually not difficult for beginners.

What You'll Need

❖ **Materials**

2 Balloons that are 2 inches wide and 60 inches long (known as 260 balloons)

Instructions

1. **Start the Monkey Balloon Animal**

   Inflate one balloon, leaving about 6 inches not inflated at the end. Knot the end. Then, make a basic twist about an inch from the knotted end. This forms the nose of the monkey.

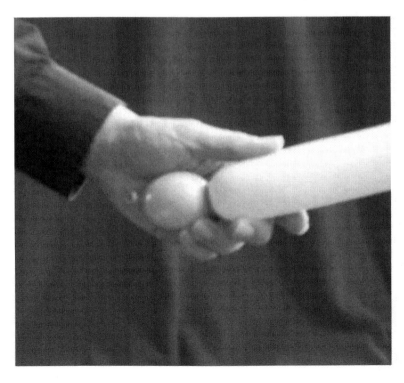

2. Form the Head

Make a small pinch twist about an inch in length just after the monkey nose. This forms one ear of the monkey.

Next, make a basic twist that's about 1 1/2 inches long to create the monkey's forehead.

Then, make another pinch twist about an inch in length to match the first one to form the second ear.

3. Finish the Head

Align the first basic twist (marked "A" in the photo below) with the rest of the remaining balloon (marked "B"). Then, twist the two pinch twists together. To do so, hold and twist the two pinch twists and the basic twist between them as a single unit. This finishes forming the monkey's head.

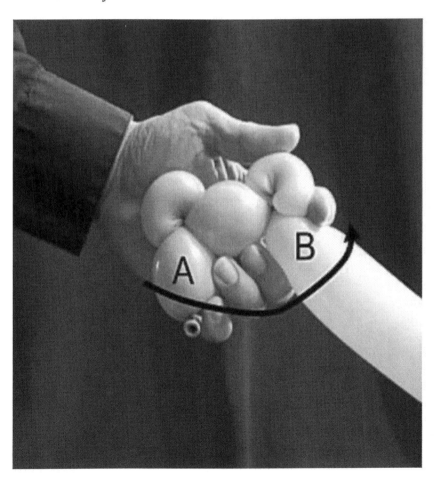

4. Check Out Your Monkey's Head

This is what the monkey's head should look like.

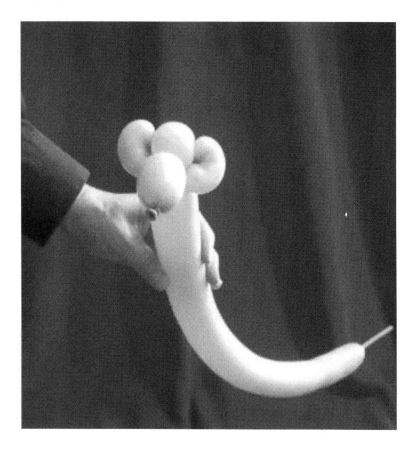

5. Form the Monkey's Arms

Now, it's time to create the monkey's body. Make two basic balloon twists below the head that are each about 2 inches long to form the monkey's arms. Create a lock twist to hold the arms together.

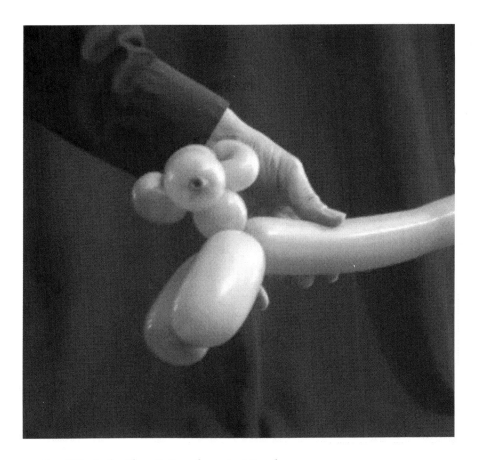

6. Finish the Monkey's Body

Make three more basic balloon twists that are each about 2 inches. The first twist forms the monkey's body. And the second and third twists form the monkey's legs. The remaining balloon segment creates the tail. Finally, do a lock twist to hold the body and legs together.

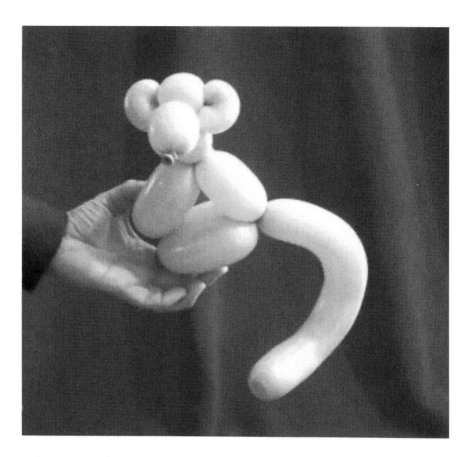

7. Finish the Monkey Balloon Animal

Inflate a second balloon to use as a pole. Slide the monkey onto the pole through its legs and arms, and enjoy your balloon animal.

Tip

If you wish, you can inflate a green balloon and twist it to add "leaves" to the top of a brown balloon pole, turning it into a palm tree for your monkey to hold. You also can opt to have your monkey hold a small yellow balloon like a banana. Once you have the monkey shape down, you can get creative with the various details.

How To Make a Balloon Butterfly

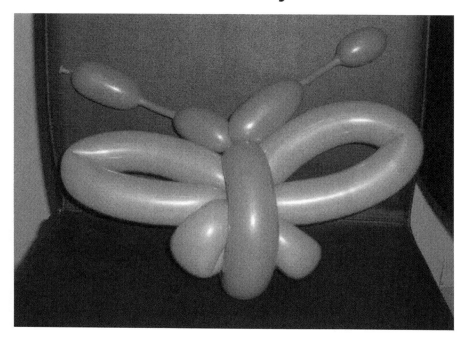

How to create balloon butterflies, frequently made in a creative and explained way. Be that as it may, this specific model rushes to make in a line work, and moreover, it dependably passes on the lightweight and straightforward magnificence of this small animal.

To make the butterfly balloon animal you will need:

- Long balloons
- A balloon hand pump

- Balloon tape for hanging butterflies on the wall

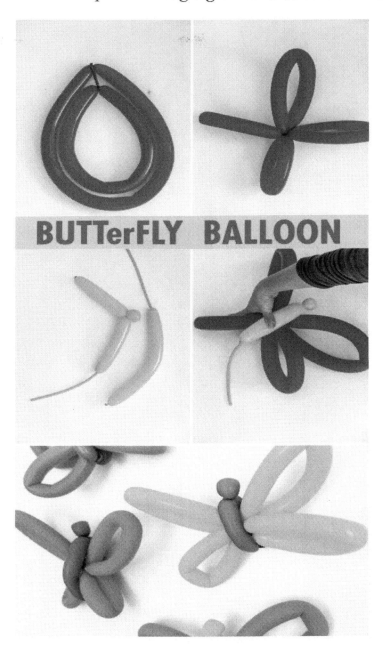

How To Make A Butterfly Balloon Animal

To make a butterfly balloon animal we want to start with the wings first!

Having the wings created to give the base to the butterfly balloon and will help create the fluttering look you are after.

- ❖ **To make the butterfly wings:**

    1. Blow up two balloons of the same color. One at full length and one a little shorter. Tie each balloon into a loop.

        You will want to use a hand balloon pump for this. I don't know if you've ever tried blowing up these long balloons without a pump, but it will literally take your breath away. Save your lungs... use a pump!

    2. Place the smaller loop inside the larger loop. With your right hand hold the knots and with your left hand pull the loops to find the centers.

        Push your left hand to your right hand and twist the balloons a few times around themselves.

3. Do final twist to make sure the larger "wings" are positioned above the smaller "wings".

❖ **To make the butterfly balloon animal body:**

4. Blow up a contrasting balloon about 1.5'. Knot at the end.

5. Find the middle and make a twist to create ahead.

❖ **To finish off making the butterfly balloon animal**

6. Place the body over the wings and tie the ends together. Tuck (or trim) the long end to complete the butterfly balloon.

How to make a balloon hat

Materials: a balloon and an air pump.

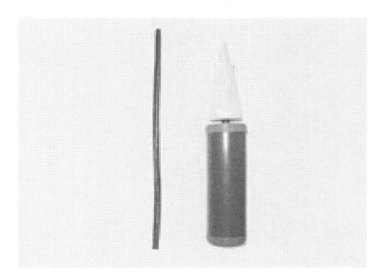

Instruction

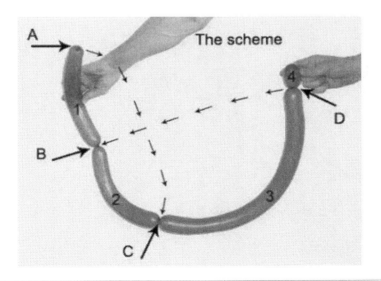

1. Inflate a balloon leaving up to 1/2 inch of the flat tail (Pic 1).

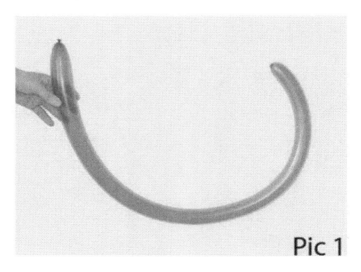

2. Twist the first bubble half the size of the head of the person you are making the hat for. Use the inflated balloon to measure the size of the head by making a loop around the head (Pic 2 and 3).

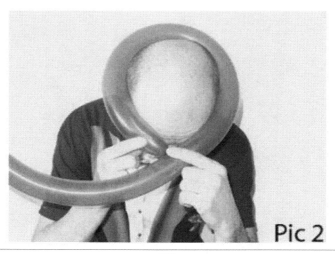

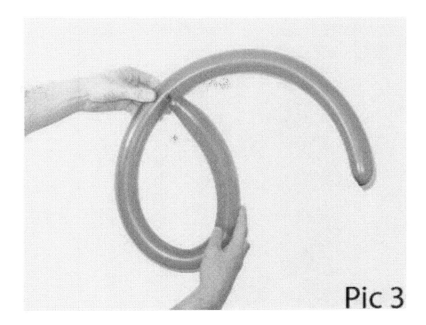

Pic 3

3. Find half of the loop (Pic 4).

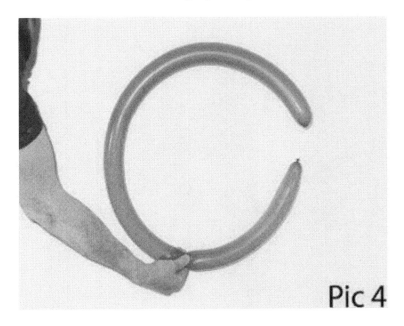

Pic 4

4. Twist the first bubble at this point (Pic 5). It's the point B on the scheme.

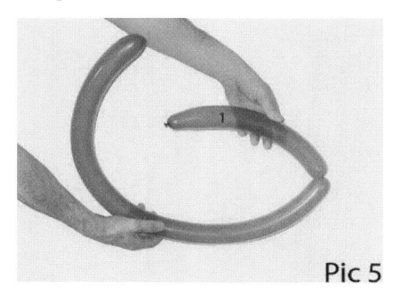

5. Twist the second bubble the same size as the first bubble (Pic 6 and 7).

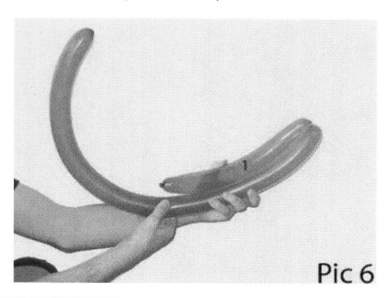

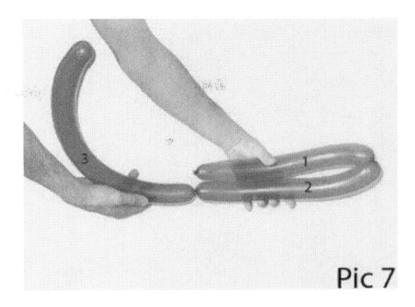

Pic 7

6. Lock both ends of the chain of the two (the 1st and the 2nd) bubbles in one lock twist (Pic 8). This step is marked with arrows between points A and C one the scheme.

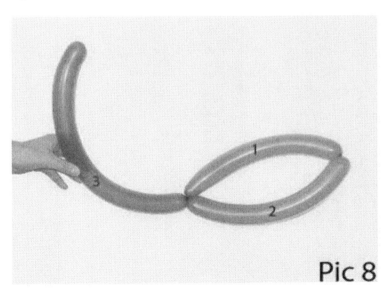

Pic 8

7. Twist the third bubble of any size, but make sure to make the fourth three−inch bubble at the end of the balloon (Pic 9).

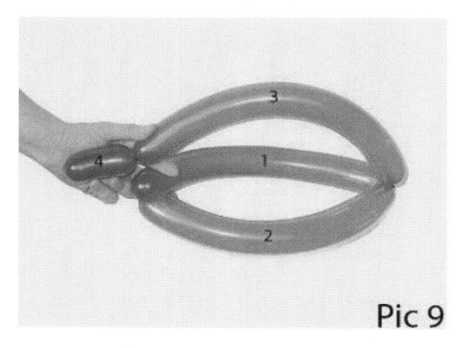

Pic 9

8. Lock the free end of the third bubble between the first and second bubbles (Pic 10 through 12). This step is marked with arrows between points B and D on the scheme. Congratulations, you have made the hat by using the bird body fold/twist.

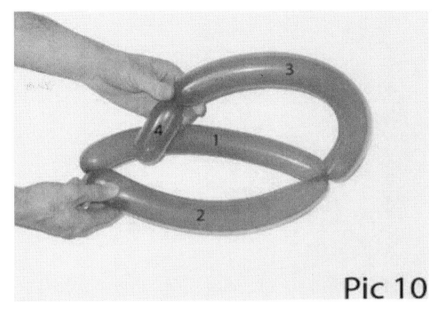

Pic 10

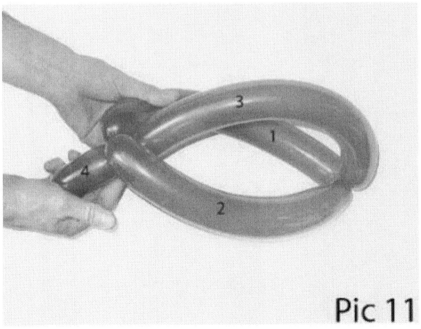

Pic 11

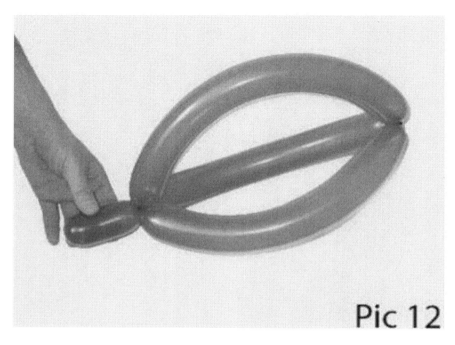

Pic 12

9. It's a basic hat (Pic 13 and 14). You may attach any other balloon sculpture to the hat. You can use this hat to make a flower. You can attach two hats together to make a pumpkin. Have fun and happy twisting :)

Pic 13

Pic 14

How to make a balloon penguin

Materials: three balloons; an air pump; a permanent marker and scissors.

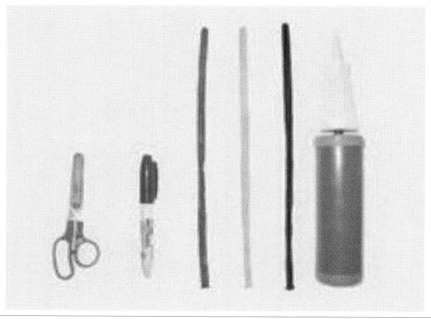

Step-By-Step Photo Guide

1. Inflate a white balloon leaving a margin at the end of slightly more than the width of a hand. Then tie the knot.

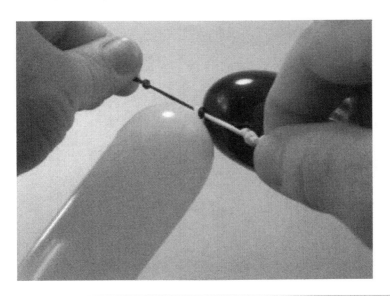

2. Do likewise with a black balloon and tie the knotted end of each balloon together.

3. With the white balloon, make a first oval bubble about three fingers wide.

4. Make a second, identical bubble, following the first.

5. Make a second, identical bubble, following the first.

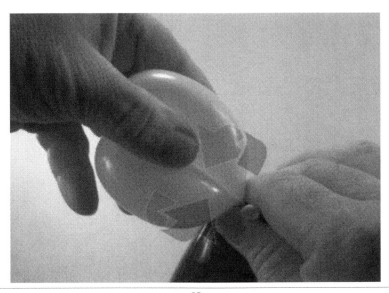

6. Twist the bubbles several times around their base to keep them in place. We already have our penguin's eyes!

7. Roll the black balloon along the groove located between the two white bubbles. In this way, shape a wide black loop and bring its base to the base of the two white bubbles.

8. Twist the two white bubbles and the black loop several times around their base to keep them in place. We've just made the head of our penguin.

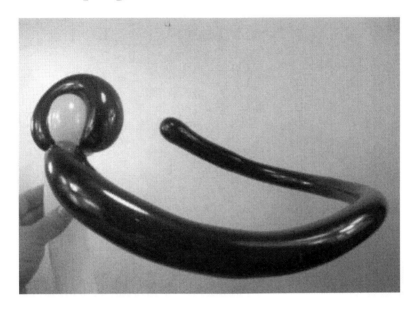

9. Push the air to the end of the remaining portion of black balloon (don't bother with the remaining portion of white balloon for the moment), you should get a shape similar to this one.

10. Twist the two white bubbles and the black loop several times around their base to keep them in place. We've just made the head of our penguin.

11. Push the air to the end of the remaining portion of black balloon (don't bother with the remaining portion of white balloon for the moment), you should get a shape similar to this one.

12. Make a zigzag with the rest of the black balloon so that the last segment is slightly longer than the first two. Make a mental note of the position of each of the two bends thus formed.

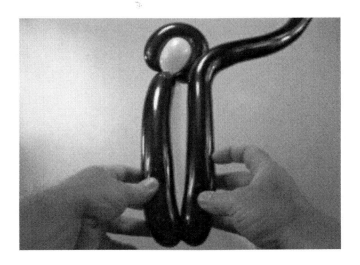

13. Make a first long bubble at the first bend formed by the zigzag.

14. Then make a second long bubble, identical to the first, normally it should fall more or less at the second bend formed by the zigzag.

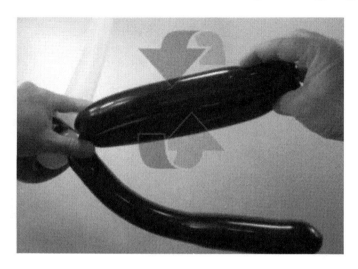

15. Twist the two large black bubbles around their base several times to block them at the base of Tux's head.

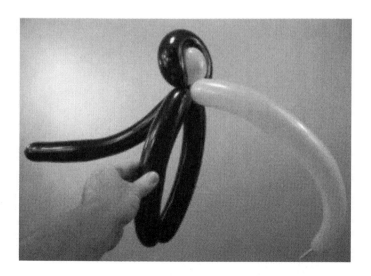

16. You should now have a shape resembling this one, with at the center, under the head, the two wings we've just created (the two long black bubbles).

17. With what's left of the black balloon, make a bubble that's shorter than the previous two. Doing so you will also get one final bubble that should be wedged between the two wings.

18. Then roll this last bubble several times between the wings to keep everything firmly in place. You can now make out Tux's head, wings, back and tail.

19. Go back to the white balloon and form a small, round bubble at the base of Tux's head.

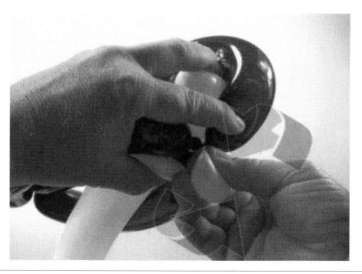

20. Make this bubble into a pinch-twist which will enable us to keep Tux's head firmly in place on top of its back and shoulders (or rather its back and wings).

21. Notice that the rest of the white balloon is naturally located under the pinch-twist.

22. You will have to feed it through to the other side, so that we can use it to make Tux's belly.

23. Push the air in the white balloon a bit towards the end, and shape a large bubble for the belly which should look a little rounded.
24. You will have to feed it through to the other side, so that we can use it to make Tux's belly.

25. Push the air in the white balloon a bit towards the end, and shape a large bubble for the belly which should look a little rounded.

26. Then finish pushing the air all the way to the end of the white balloon so that there is no remaining length of empty balloon.

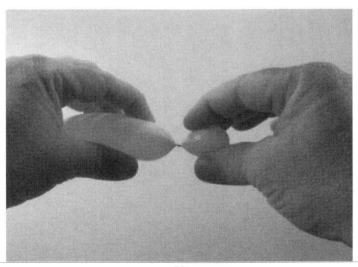

27. Make a small bubble at the tip of the white balloon.

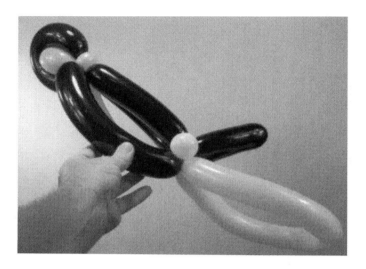

28. Then wedge the small white bubble into the joint common to the base of the wings, the base of the back, and the tail. It doesn't matter which side the bubble is sticking out from for now. Having done this, we get a large loop.

29. We are now going to learn how to divide one big loop into two smaller loops. To do this, twist the large white loop into two equal parts and take note of the central mark.

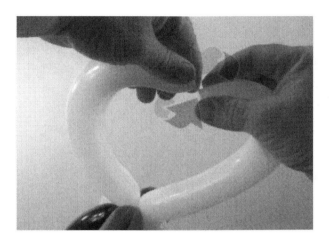

30. At the level of this mark, press the balloon to form two large bubbles then hold one of the bubbles firmly in one hand while twisting the other bubble around its base with the other hand, to divide the loop into two equal parts.

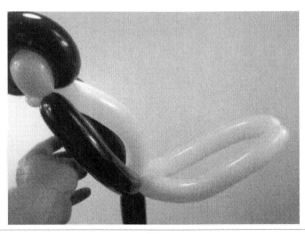

31. This way, you get two distinct bubbles. Now let's see how to turn both of them into loops.

32. It's very simple! All you need to do is bring the creases formed at the ends of each bubble together, and thus naturally shape two new (smaller) loops.

33. Hold one of the loops firmly in one hand while twisting the other loop around its base with your other hand to keep them both in place.

34. Finally, place the small bubble, that we had set aside, right between the two loops. We have just made two wide, webbed feet, on which Tux can now stand securely.

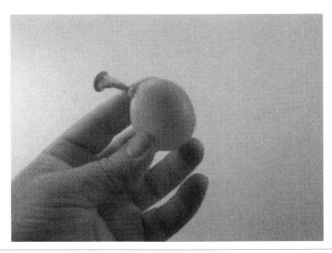

35. We are almost finished. All that's left now is the beak! For this, **very lightly** inflate a small round balloon, preferably yellow

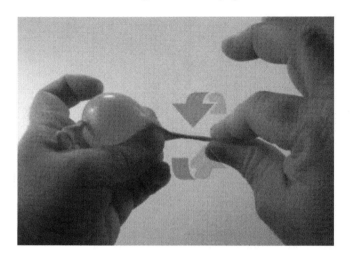

36. Press on the tip of the balloon and, gripping the latex, twist the tip a little so that the air leaves it completely and pushes against the knotted end of the balloon.

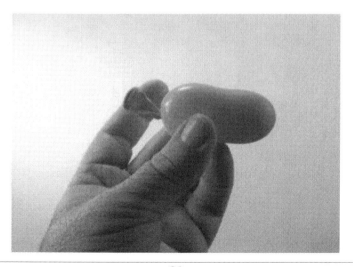

37. Gently let go of the latex to enable the air to come back gradually into the balloon, which should now be elongated or at the very least oval.

38. Wedge the knotted end of the beak at the base of the head. Lastly, draw on the eyes, and round out the shapes of Tux's wings, back and stomach to put the finishing touches on this sculpture.

And that's all there is to it!

Made in the USA
Columbia, SC
28 November 2021